MW00930747

Published by Collins
An imprint of HarperCollins Publishers
Westerhill Road, Bishopbriggs,
Glasgow G64 2QT

HarperCollins Publishers
1st Floor, Watermarque Building,
Ringsend Road, Dublin 4, Ireland

www.harpercollins.co.uk

© HarperCollins Publishers 2022

Collins® is a registered trademark of HarperCollins
Publishers Ltd.

All images © Shutterstock.com

Text © Becky Goddard-Hill

Cover title font © Kia Marie Hunt

Cover author name font © Clare Forrest

All rights reserved. No part of this publication may be
reproduced, stored in a retrieval system, or transmitted,
in any form or by any means, electronic, mechanical,
photocopying, recording or otherwise without the prior
permission in writing of the Publisher and copyright
owners. The contents of this publication are believed
correct at the time of printing. Nevertheless the Publisher
can accept no responsibility for errors or omissions,
changes in the detail given or for any expense or loss
thereby caused.

A catalogue record for this book is available from the
British Library.

978-0-00-854524-6

Printed in India

10 9 8 7 6 5 4 3 2 1

I dedicate this book
to my gorgeous Dad
who made the world
laugh every day.

MIX
Paper from
responsible sources
FSC™ C007454

FSC
www.fsc.org

This book is produced from independently certified FSC™ paper
to ensure responsible forest management.

For more information visit: www.harpercollins.co.uk/green

Collins

365 Days of Happy

Becky Goddard-Hill

Happy

It is in your POWER to make YOURSELF, other PEOPLE, and the planet HAPPIER each and every day. YOUR THOUGHTS, your ACTIONS and YOUR CHOICES can make all the difference when it comes to

HAPPINESS.

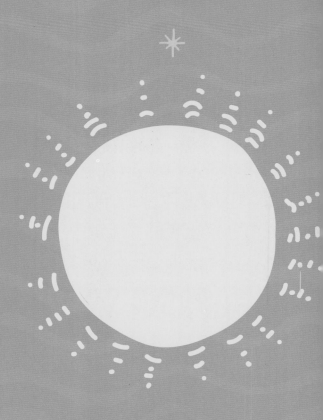

Are you ready to boost your happiness every day of the year?

Try out the simple activities throughout your day or the whole week through and read the inspirational quotes all about being happy. The affirmations are positive statements that you might want to repeat to yourself or say aloud to strengthen your belief in them.

The book is perfect for opening at the beginning of your day, before you go to bed or anytime!

A New Start

1

This book is about to send you off on a journey to greater happiness. Start it off well by thinking of something amazing you are going to make happen during the year ahead of you.

State it out loud and write it down as well to give it a better chance of success.

2

" Whatever YOU CAN DO, or DREAM YOU CAN, begin it. Boldness has genius, power, and magic in it. "

Goethe

3

" The big question is whether you are going to be able to say a hearty yes to your adventure. "

Joseph Campbell

4 "Each NEW DAY
is a blank page
in the diary of
your life. The
secret of success
is in turning that
diary into the
best story you
possibly can."

Douglas Pagels

"Every moment is 5 a fresh beginning."

T.S. Eliot

6 I will fill the year ahead with ADVENTURES.

7 I am on a JOURNEY to happiness.

HAVE A GOOD MORNING

8 Each day this week use a different language to say good morning to your family. It is an interesting, fun and friendly way to start the day.

French - *Bonjour*   Indonesian – *Selamat pagi*

Hebrew - Shalom

Swedish – God morgon   Italian – Buongiorno

Portuguese – bom dia   WELSH – BORE DA

If you want to pronounce them perfectly, ask your grown up to help you search on the internet.

9

" If you want to make your dreams come true, the first thing you have to do is wake up. "

J.M. Power

10

" When writing the story of your life, don't let anyone else hold the pen. "

11

" Someday is
not a day
of the week. "

Denise Brennan-Nelson

12

" Give **EVERY DAY** the
chance to become
the most
BEAUTIFUL DAY
of your life. "

Mark Twain

I will make the most of this morning. 13

14 I START each day FULL of JOY!

What is happiness?

15 Ask someone what they think happiness is. Share your thoughts too. It is really interesting to find we can have such different views about the same idea and it is important to know what it means to you.

16

I will do more of what makes ME HAPPY.

17

" Happiness is not a state to arrive at, but a manner of traveling. "

Margaret Lee Runbeck

18 "RULES for HAPPINESS: something to do, someone to love, something to hope for."

IMMANUEL KANT

19 "A happy life is just a string of happy **MOMENTS**."

"Happiness is when what **20** you think, what you say, and what you do are in harmony."

21 I **CREATE** my own happy.

COLLECT BEAUTIFUL MOMENTS

22

At the end of today, share with your family 3 happy moments from your day. Try and take a mental photograph of them as they happen so you remember them to share them later.

23

I will fill today with lovely moments.

24

"When we pause and appreciate a moment it makes it even more special. When we remember that moment later it makes us happy all over again."

25

"Keep SMILING, because life is a BEAUTIFUL THING and there's so much to SMILE about."

※ Marilyn Monroe

I am thankful for EVERY MOMENT of HAPPINESS.

26

27

> **Be happy in the moment, that's enough. Each moment is all we need, not more.**

Mother Teresa

28

> **There is no path to happiness, happiness is the path.**

Buddha

Changing Your Mood

29

If you want to change your mood today simply close your eyes. Think about a party you have had or been to that was full of fun. Can you see it? Are you smiling? Your mind is so powerful you can change how you feel just with your thoughts. You can do this whenever you need to.

A HAPPY PLACE IS ALWAYS JUST A MEMORY AWAY AND CAN TOTALLY CHANGE YOUR MOOD.

30

"If YOU don't LIKE something, change it. If YOU can't CHANGE it, CHANGE YOUR ATTITUDE."

Maya Angelou

31

I choose my HAPPY MOOD.

32 "It's **BEEN** my experience tha you can nearly always **ENJOY** things if you make up your mind firmly that you will."

 Anne Shirley, *Anne of Green Gables*

33 "With the new day comes new strength and **NEW THOUGHTS.**"

Eleanor Roosevelt

"Today is my new **34** favourite day."

35 I have the **POWER** to change how I feel.

Being Your Own Best Friend

36 Do something SUPER kind for yourself today. Perhaps you could take a big bubble bath, watch your favourite TV show, or give yourself a host of compliments as you look in the mirror. Do something kind for yourself EVERY day this week.

37

The only thing that will make you happy is being happy with who you are.

Goldie Hawn

38

Never put the key to your happiness in someone else's pocket.

39

"The best friend you will ever find is you."

Debasish Mridha

40

I am MY OWN best FRIEND.

'Fall head over heels in love with YOURSELF. ' 41

42 I LOVE myself.

ACTION

43

Decide on a goal that will make you happy and then plan small steps to get you there. This week, make a start on putting that plan into action. Take that first step — what will it be?

44

"The most effective way to do it is to do it."

Amelia Earhart

   45

I will do great things today.

46

"The secret of getting ahead is getting started."

Mark Twain

HAPPINESS is not **47** something **READY** made. It comes from your **OWN** **ACTIONS.**"

Dalai Lama

"One DAY or DAY one? It's YOUR CHOICE." 48

49 I CAN reach my GOALS.

Mindset

50 ♪

Make up your mind to be as happy as you can be this week and to see the good in every day. Start right now.

WHAT IS GOOD ABOUT TODAY?

51

TODAY IS A BEAUTIFUL DAY.

52

" When I went to school, they asked me what I wanted to be when I grew up. I wrote down happy. "

53

"The HAPPIEST people don't have the best of everything they just make the BEST OF EVERYTHING."

54 "Most folks are about as happy as they make their minds up to be."

55 "Happiness depends upon OURSELVES."

Aristotle

56 I am CONTENT.

NOW

57

Sit quietly and really pay attention. Name...

- 5 things you can see,
- 4 things you can hear,
- 3 things you can touch,
- 2 things you can smell and
- 1 thing you can taste.

Be in the moment and appreciate exactly where you are.

58

66 *Happiness, not in another place but this place...not for another hour, but this hour.* 99

Walt Whitman

I am thankful for my life right now.

59

60

" Forever is composed of nows. "

Emily Dickinson

61

"Do not set aside your **HAPPINESS**. Do not wait to be happy in the future. The best time to be **HAPPY** is always now."

Roy T. Bennett

62 I am wonderful just as I am.

63 "WHY go for a happy ending when you can have a happy NOW?"

Making Yourself Happy

Make a list of 10 things that make you happy – think about places, people, hobbies, food, pets, games ...anything!

64

65

I am in charge of MY own HAPPINESS.

66

"Happiness is your own treasure because it lies within you."

Prem Rawat

67 "BE the TYPE OF PERSON you want to meet."

"Get lost in what you love." 68

"Learn to value yourself, which means: fight for your happiness." 69

Ayn Rand

70 **I am MY OWN best friend.**

CREATING YOUR OWN HAPPY

71

Make a planner for the week and against each day plan in one thing you KNOW will make you happy.

72

I will fill my day with happiness.

"Design a life you love to live." **73**

74

" It is not how much we have, but how much we enjoy, that makes happiness. "

Charles Spurgeon

75

" Remember **HAPPINESS** doesn't depend upon who you are or what you have, it depends **SOLELY** on what you think. "

Dale Carnegie

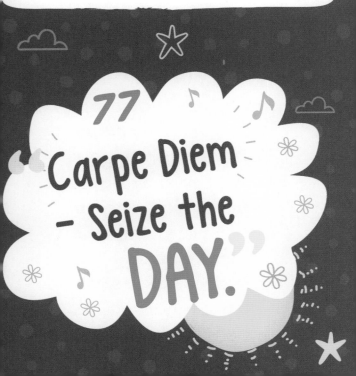

I can make **76** MYSELF HAPPY.

77

"Carpe Diem – Seize the DAY."

Happy Thoughts

78 ☆

Close your eyes and remember a time and place that made you feel amazing. Focus on what you could see and hear, how you felt and all the colours. You can think happy thoughts whenever you choose.

79

"Your MIND is a powerful thing. When YOU fill it with POSITIVE thoughts, YOUR LIFE will start to CHANGE."

♪ **80**

I think happy THOUGHTS.

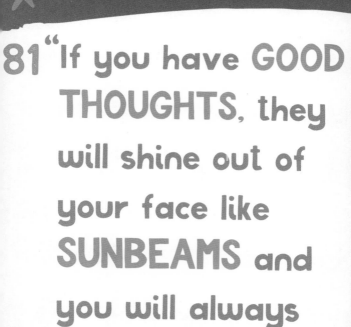

81 "If you have GOOD THOUGHTS, they will shine out of your face like SUNBEAMS and you will always look lovely."

Roald Dahl

82 "There are so many beautiful reasons TO BE HAPPY."

83 "If you tell yourself you feel fine, you will."

Jodi Picoult

84 I am in a GOOD MOOD.

Don't Worry Be Happy

85

Worries can either be released or overcome. Think of two worries you have; one you can do something about and one you can't. Imagine the one you can't do anything about is inside a big red balloon. Take yourself outside and let that balloon go high above the clouds and take your worry with it. There is no point going over and over a worry you cannot change.

For the one you can do something about sit and talk it through with someone wise and make a plan to help things get better.

86

"You are in control of your worries. They are not in control of you."

87

I won't worry about things I can't control.

88

"Don't let yesterday take up too much of today."

Will Rogers

89

"WORRY is like a ROCKING CHAIR: it gives you something to do but never gets you anywhere."

Erma Bombeck

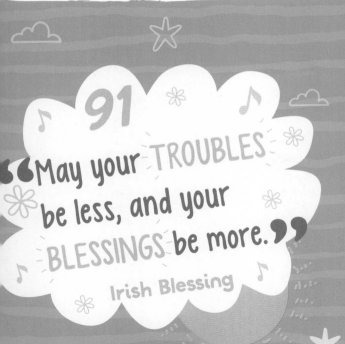

I have the power to change **MY STORY.** 90

91

"May your TROUBLES be less, and your BLESSINGS be more."

Irish Blessing

SIMPLICITY

92

Can you think of 10 everyday things that make you happy? Things such as green grass, a slice of toast, red buses, sunshine and bees.

93

"I am satisfied. I see, dance, laugh, sing."

Walt Whitman

94

I am content and happy with all I have.

95

"Very little is needed to make a happy life; it is all within yourself, in your way of thinking."

Marcus Aurelius

"NATURE, books, music, love for one's NEIGHBOUR — such is my idea of HAPPINESS."

96

Leo Tolstoy

I ENJOY the simple THINGS. **97**

98

"You can't buy happiness, but you can buy ICE CREAM. And that's kind of the same thing."

Friends

99 ♪

Imagine your 3 favourite friends lined up in front of you and imagine yourself telling each one of them why they are special to you. Now, maybe you could do this for real? Good friends are precious, and they need to know how much you appreciate them.

100

I AM THANKFUL FOR MY FRIENDSHIPS.

101

"A good friend knows all your stories. A best friend helped you create them."

102

"Many people will WALK in  and out of your life, but only true friends will leave footprints in your HEART."

Eleanor Roosevelt

103 "Good friends are like stars, you don't always see them, but you know they're always there."

104 "Friendship isn't a big thing — it's a million little things."
Paulo Coelho

105 I let my FRIENDS know how much I care.

NURTURE NATURE

106

Give something back to nature today. Plant a seed perhaps or leave out some water for the birds. Nurture nature as it nurtures you.

107

I respect and protect all living things.

108

"You are never too small to make a difference."

Greta Thunberg

"LOVE the **WORLD** as your own self; then you can **TRULY** care for all things.**"**

Lao Tzu

"If you truly LOVE nature, you will find beauty everywhere."

Laura Ingalls Wilder

I am a nature nurturer. 111

112

"Make every day Earth Day."

Being Unique

113

Using the fingers on your hand, count up 5 things that make you unique and special. Could you do the other hand too?

114

I have MANY special QUALITIES.

115

" Today you are you, that is truer than true. There is no one alive who is you-er than you. "

Dr. Seuss

☆ 116

"Be yourself;
EVERYONE
else is already
TAKEN."

117 "The things that make me different are the things that make me."

Piglet, *Winnie-the-Pooh*

118 "Being different isn't a bad thing. It means you're brave enough to be yourself."

119 I am one of a **KIND**.

HUGS

120

Open your arms wide and take a deep breath. Then fold your arms around your body, around your tummy or chest, and give yourself a squeeze. Then gently rock yourself from side to side for 10 seconds. **CONSIDER YOURSELF HUGGED!**

121

I can hug myself.

122

"A hug is always the right size."

123

"The good thing about hugs: when you give one, you get one."

Diana Rowland

124

"SOMETIMES it's better to put LOVE into HUGS than to put it into words."

Positivity

127

Keep a diary this week and write down 3 brilliant things that happen each day.

128

"When it **RAINS**, look for **RAINBOWS**; when it's **DARK**, look for **STARS**."

129

I am full of **POSITIVITY**.

"Some PEOPLE could look at a MUD PUDDLE and see an ocean with SHIPS."

130

Zora Neale Hurston

131 I'm choosing to have a **BRILLIANT DAY.**

"Just think of lovely things and your heart will fly on wings." **132**

Peter Pan, *Peter Pan*

133 "Put on your **POSITIVE PANTS!**"

Grow

134

Make a plan this week to improve something that matters to you. You grow and change all the time. Keep moving forward to be the best you that you can be.

135

"Mighty oaks from little acorns grow."

136

I am growing every day in every way.

137

"Look in the mirror. That's your competition."

138

"Don't try to be PERFECT. Just try to be BETTER than you were YESTERDAY."

I can push **MYSELF.** 139

140
"In order to **BLOOM** you must **GROW.**"

TRICKY TIMES

141

Think of something you are finding hard and rather than focus on how tough it is ask yourself this – what could make things better? Even if you only come up with a tiny thing that will help, it will move you from being a problem dweller to a problem solver and towards happier times.

If you can't think of anything that would make it better, ask someone to help you.

142

"A problem is a chance for you to do your best."

Duke Ellington

143

I can cope with difficult things.

144

" Every day may not be good... but there's something good in every day. "

Alice Morse Earle

145

" Even in the MUD and SCUM of things, something always, always SINGS. "

Ralph Waldo Emerson

If I fall, I get back up. **146**

147

"HAPPINESS is like WAVES. It will come around again."

Confidence

148 ♪

Pick something new to try this week (perhaps baking, juggling, making a new friend). Set your goal and give it a really good go.

149

I can do HARD things.

150

"Believe you can and you're halfway there."

Theodore Roosevelt

151

"The question ISN'T WHO is going to let me it's who is going to STOP ME."

152 " If you hear a voice within you say you cannot paint, then by all means paint and that voice will be silenced. "

Vincent Van Gogh

153 I have faith in **MYSELF.**

154 "Not here to be **AVERAGE** – here to be awesome."

COURAGE

155

Who is your superhero? Is it Harriet Tubman or Nelson Mandela, or perhaps Marcus Rashford or Joan of Arc? Read a story about someone inspirational and you will find their courage will inspire you. You could ask your friends and family to share who their heroes are and why as well.

"*Dance like nobody's* (156) *watching.*"

(157)

I will always find a way.

158

"I am not afraid of STORMS, for I am learning how to sail my ship."

Amy March, *Little Women*

159

"You're BRAVER than you believe, and STRONGER than you seem, and SMARTER than you think."

Christopher Robin, *Pooh's Grand Adventure*

I am full of courage. 160

161

"Be who you were created to be, and you will set the world on FIRE."

St. Catherine of Siena

Follow Your Dreams

♪ **162**

Close your eyes and think about one of your dreams, a dream you know you could achieve if you worked really hard. See it coming true as if you are watching it on a TV screen. Notice all the colours and the sounds too. Imagine how amazing it feels to achieve it.

Now open your eyes. What's the very first step? Make it happen. Ask for the help you need. Believe in yourself.

163

"The journey of a thousand miles begins with a single step."

Lao Tzu

164 "THE FUTURE belongs to those who believe in the beauty of their DREAMS."

Eleanor Roosevelt

"Dreams, to come true, need a good story. So go live one." Vironika Tugaleva 165

☆ I believe in my ♪ 166 **DREAMS.**

167

"I can reach for the STARS!"

☆　☆　☆

"Go confidently in the direction of your dreams! Live the life you've imagined."

168 Henry David Thoreau

HAVING FUN

169

Find a brilliant joke and share it with at least 3 people today. Doesn't it feel great to make people laugh? ★

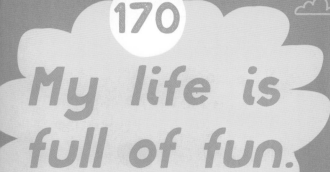

170

My life is full of fun.

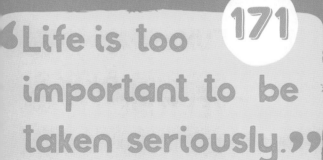

171

"Life is too important to be taken seriously."

172

"We don't laugh because we're happy – we're happy because we laugh."

William James

173

"HAVE FUN, even if it's not the same KIND of fun EVERYONE else is having."

I find reasons to laugh EVERY DAY.

174

175

"Find ecstasy in life;
the mere sense of
LIVING is joy enough."

Emily Dickinson

Hope

176

Have a go at answering these 3 questions: What do you hope for yourself? What do you hope for for your family? What do you hope for the world?

I believe that DREAMS come 177 TRUE.

"Learn from yesterday, live for today, hope for tomorrow." 178

179

"**OPTIMISM**
is the faith ☆
that leads to
ACHIEVEMENT."

Helen Keller

"There is always light **180** behind the CLOUDS."

Marmee, *Little Women*

"If you can dream it, you can do it."

181

Walt Disney

☆ ⁀I am ⁀ **182** FULL OF HOPE.

Happy Thoughts

183

List your 5 favourite things to do and your 5 favourite places to go. Thinking of good things will always make you smile.

184

"If you can't find the sunshine, be the sunshine."

I can always **185** think about happy things.

186

"When you love what you have, you have everything you need."

187

"Keep your FACE to the SUN and you will never see the SHADOWS."

66 **May your day be filled with good thoughts, kind people, and happy moments.** 99 **188**

I am **189**
THANKFUL
for all that is
good in my life.

GRATITUDE

190

Each day this week share 3 things you are grateful for over dinner. Notice how happy it makes you to acknowledge and remember all that has made you smile.

191

❝When eating fruit, remember the one who planted the tree.❞

Vietnamese proverb

I have so many good things in my life.

192

193

" Feeling gratitude and not expressing it is like **wrapping** a present and not giving it. "

William Arthur Ward

194

" The best and most **BEAUTIFUL** things in this world cannot be seen or even heard, but must be felt with the **HEART**. "

Helen Keller

Adventures

197

If you were to go on an amazing adventure, where would you go? What would you do? And who would be with you? Could you draw this, write it up as a story or tell someone all about it to really bring it to life?

198

I have MANY adventures ahead. ♪

199

"Life is a great big canvas; throw all the paint you can on it."

Danny Kaye

200

"All life is an
EXPERIMENT.
The more experiment
you make, the
BETTER.

Ralph Waldo Emerson

201 " The purpose of life is to live it, to taste experience to the utmost, to reach out eagerly and without fear for newer and richer experience. "

Eleanor Roosevelt

202 I am an EXPLORER.

203 "What makes you feel ALIVE? Do more of that."

LOVE

204

Think of 3 people you love and who you know love you too. Put your hand on your heart and one by one imagine their faces, give them a smile and a silent thank you.

Feel how steady and slowly your heart is beating. Love makes us feel all kinds of good.

The greatest thing you'll ever learn is to love and be loved in return.

205

Nat King Cole

206

I have lots of love to give.

207

" There is only one HAPPINESS in this life, to love and be loved. "

George Sand

208

" Spread LOVE everywhere you go. Let no one ever come to YOU without leaving happier. "

Mother Teresa

I am loved. 209

210

"Love is sharing your popcorn."

Charles Schultz

Giving

211

Give something lovely away today. It could be a piece of art or a cake, a hug or a story. It could be a toy you once loved. Notice how good that felt for both you and the receiver.

212
I HAVE so much to GIVE.

213
"No one has ever become poor from giving."

Anne Frank

214

"Those who are **HAPPIEST** are those who do the most for **OTHERS.**"

Booker T. Washington

"The more I give to the world, the more I get." 215

" Since you get more joy out of giving joy to others, you should put a good deal of thought into the happiness that you are able to give. "
216
Eleanor Roosevelt

"For it is in giving that we receive." ♪
St. Francis of Assisi 217

HAPPINESS
SPREADS

Make it your mission today to brighten every situation with a smile, a laugh or a kind deed and see your happiness spread.

218

219

My smile makes others smile.

220

"Whoever is happy will make others happy "

Anne Frank

221

"To get the full value of joy you must have someone to divide it with."

Mark Twain

222

"No **KIND** action ever stops with itself. One **KIND** action leads to another."

Amelia Earhart

I spread JOY WHEREVER I go. ✳ **223**

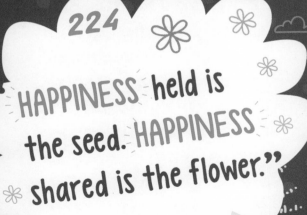

224

"**HAPPINESS** held is the seed. **HAPPINESS** shared is the flower."

Giving Thanks

225

Have a think about who you need to say thank you to...perhaps a friend, a coach, or perhaps your grandparents. Do something about it today, ring them up, write them a note or send an email. Let them know how you very much appreciate them.

I SAY THANK YOU OFTEN.

"Give thanks for a little and you will find a lot."

Hansa proverb

228

"When I started counting my **BLESSINGS,** my whole life turned around

 Willie Nelson

"Live today with an **229**
ATTITUDE of GRATITUDE."

"The more you praise and celebrate your life, the more there is in life to celebrate."

230 Oprah Winfrey

I'm **231**
grateful for
MY FAMILY AND FRIENDS.

Making Others Happy

232

Think of something specific you can do today to make someone else happy. Could you help your grown-up load the dishwasher or play your sibling's favourite game. Could you offer to help your neighbour as they clean their car? Making someone else happy will make you feel happy too.

233

"If you would be loved, love, and be loveable."

Benjamin Franklin

234

I have happiness to share.

235

"Happiness is the only thing that multiplies when you share it."
Albert Schweitzer

236

"Those who are HAPPIEST are those who do the most for OTHERS."
Booker T. Washington

237

I bring other PEOPLE JOY.

238

"When someone else's HAPPINESS is your HAPPINESS, that's love"

Lana Del Rey

ENCOURAGING OTHERS

Have a think about your family and friends. Who needs cheering on with something? Maybe your sibling has an exam coming up or one of your friends has a football match – could you send them a message or make them a card? Find a way to let them know you are supporting them.

239

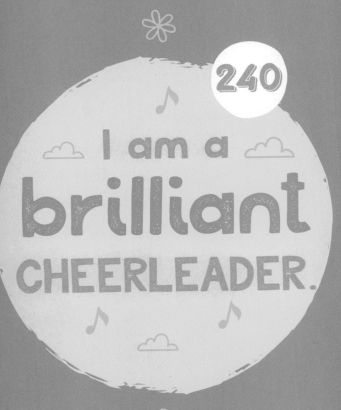

240

I am a
brilliant
CHEERLEADER.

241

"A little consideration, a little thought for others, makes all the difference. Be somebody who makes everybody feel like somebody."

I ENJOY 242 encouraging others.

"We rise by LIFTING others." 243

"A FRIEND is someone who HELPS you up when YOU'RE DOWN, and if they can't, they LAY DOWN beside you and listen."

"The best way to cheer yourself up is to try to cheer someone else up."

245

Mark Twain

Friendship

♪ 246

Think about 5 things you look for in a friend. Write them on a piece of paper and look at them each morning. Spend each day this week being all of those things yourself.

247
I am a wonderful FRIEND.

248
"A friend is someone who makes it easy to believe in yourself."

Heidi Wills

249

"There's nothing **BETTER** than a friend, unless it is a friend with **CHOCOLATE**

"It's so much more friendly with two."
250

My 251
FRIENDSHIP
is a gift.

"To have a good
FRIEND 252
you have to be one."

SPREADING JOY

Your task
this week is to be
a secret joy spreader.
Could you leave an apple
on your teacher's desk,
pop a compliment in your
friend's coat pocket or
make a bookmark and
leave it in a library
book you return?
Be creative!

253

254

"Spread happiness one smile at a time."

255

I give off good vibes.

256

I have HAPPINESS to share.

257

"If SOMEONE makes you HAPPY, make them HAPPIER."

"Be a 258
GLITTERBALL
of joy."

"ALWAYS LOOK
on the bright
side of life." 259

Play

☀ 260

Have a think about your 5 favourite games and then think who might like to play one of them with you today. Maybe they have a game to teach you too that you don't yet know?

You are never too old for a new game and there are 100's of card games, board games, puzzles, video and outdoor games to explore.

261
I LOVE TO HAVE FUN.

262
"At the end of the day, if I can say I had fun, it was a good day."
Simone Biles

263

"We don't stop **PLAYING** because we grow old; we grow old because we stop **PLAYING.**"

George Bernard Shaw

I can always find time to play. 264

265
"Today was good. Today was fun. Tomorrow is another one." Dr. Seuss

"Do at least one fun thing every day." 266

Clifford Cohen

SMILING

267

Smile at someone new each day this week and keep a tally – how many smiled back?

268

I have so many reasons to smile.

269

'Peace begins with a smile.'
Mother Teresa

270

"The HAPPIEST people seem to be those who have no particular cause for being HAPPY except that they are so."

William Ralph Inge

271

"It was only a SUNNY SMILE, and little it cost in the giving, but like MORNING LIGHT it scattered the NIGHT and made the DAY worth living."

I have a **272** BEAUTIFUL smile.

273 "Turn that FROWN upside down!"

Being a World Citizen

274

There are many people all around the world that need our care and support. Can you do something this week for a charity that helps them? Perhaps you could donate your pocket money or a toy to one of your local charity shops, or perhaps you could fundraise with a bake sale.

275

I can make the WORLD a better place.

"I believe there is only one race — the human race."

Rosa Parks

276

277

"INSTEAD of trying to be the best in the WORLD try and be the best FOR the WORLD."

I spread HAPPINESS everywhere I go. 278

"The good we do today becomes the happiness of tomorrow." 279 ♪ William James

"Happiness is 280 CONTAGIOUS. Pass it on."

Taking Care of Our Planet

281

Go outside and pick up 3 pieces of rubbish and instantly make our lovely planet look and feel better. Try and do this every day this week.

282

"Be part of the solution, not the pollution."

283

I reduce, reuse and recycle.

284

"The EARTH does not belong to us, we belong to the EARTH."

285

"We OURSELVES feel that what we are doing is just a drop in the OCEAN. But the ocean would be less because of that missing drop."

Mother Teresa

I am a caretaker of our beautiful earth. 286

287

"The EARTH is what we all have in common?"

MAKING A DIFFERENCE

288 Take a food parcel to drop off at your local food bank or a warm clothes parcel to drop off at a homeless shelter. If you don't have enough things to gift yourself, you could ask your neighbours or family members to contribute too.

289

66 Act as if what you do makes a difference, it does. 99

William James

I can make a difference to the WORLD.

290

291

"How wonderful it is that nobody need wait a single moment before starting to improve the world."

Anne Frank

292

"Always REMEMBER, you have within you the STRENGTH, the patience, and the passion to reach for the STARS, to change the WORLD."

What I do MATTERS. **293**

294
"Be the CHANGE that you wish to see in the WORLD."

Being Outdoors

295

No matter what the weather, get yourself outside today and either dance in a puddle, make snow angels, bathe in the sunshine or lie on your back and make pictures out of the clouds. There is no such thing as bad weather.

296

I am a child of the UNIVERSE.

✳

297

" Some old-fashioned things like fresh air and sunshine are hard to beat. **"**

Laura Ingalls Wilder

"The Best 8 DOCTORS:

1. Sunshine 2. Air
3. EXERCISE
4. Water 5. Diet
6. Rest
7. Laughter.
8. LOVE."

"To walk into nature **299** is to witness a thousand miracles."

Mary Davis

I am **300** GRATEFUL for the great outdoors.

"If you think sunshine brings you **HAPPINESS,** then you haven't danced **301** in the rain." ♪

HOME

Make a square by pressing your fingers and thumbs together. Now go into each room in your home and look at it through your 'lens'. What are your favourite things about each room? Sometimes we take our home for granted and it is good to look at it with fresh eyes.

302

303

"A house is made of walls and beams; a home is built with love and dreams."

304

I am GRATEFUL for my home.

305

"There's no place like HOME."

Dorothy,
The Wonderful Wizard of Oz

306

"Some PEOPLE look for a BEAUTIFUL place. Others make a place BEAUTIFUL."

Hazrat Inayat Khan

I will HELP keep MY HOME looking LOVELY. 307

308

"May your HOME always be too SMALL to hold all of your FRIENDS."

Irish saying

Relax

☆ **309**

Create a den for
yourself today, a
comfy space with
cushions and blankets
and books and snacks
and even fairy lights
if you have some.
Relaxing deeply is
deeply relaxing.

310
I am RELAXED and CONTENT.

311
"For fast-acting relief, try slowing down."

Lily Tomlin

312

"No need to **HURRY**. No need to **SPARKLE**. No need to be **ANYBODY** but **ONESELF**." ☆

Virginia Woolf

I let all my worries float away. **313**

"If you want to be happy, be." **314**
Leo Tolstoy

"Time you enjoy wasting, is not wasted." **315**
Marthe Troly-Curtin

HAPPY
BODY

316

Can you work your way up and down your body giving it thanks for all it does for you?

Maybe you could wriggle your fingers and thank them for holding a pen, or flutter your eyelashes and thank your eyes for the beautiful things they can see. Maybe you could touch your knees and say cheers for being so bendy or perhaps you want to scrunch your nose and appreciate it for smelling fresh grass and strawberries.

Our bodies are just incredible.

317

I am thankful for my body.

318

"I stand in awe of my body."
Henry David Thoreau

319
My BODY is AMAZING.

320
"There's **NO-BODY** quite like **MY-BODY.**

Happy Mind

323

Give your busy brain a break today after it has worked hard for you, talking, thinking or studying. Allow it time to rest and just fill up with lovely images. Close your eyes and listen to some relaxing music without words. What fills your mind when you do? If worries float into your mind just tell them gently to go away and focus on something you are looking forward to instead. Your brain, just like your body, needs a rest sometimes.

324

I let MY MIND rest and RELAX.

"Every great dream begins with a dreamer."

325

326

"Your MIND is the GARDEN, your thoughts are the seeds, the HARVEST can either be flowers or WEEDS."

William Wordsworth

"The secret of happiness 327 is to count your blessings while others are adding up their troubles."

William Penn

"Almost everything will work again if you unplug it for a few minutes...including you."

328 Anne Lamott

I appreciate my
AMAZING
brain. 329

Laughter

330

Find the funny today. Watch a show that makes you laugh, read a funny story or hit the joke books. Then share what has made you laugh with someone else and spread that fun around.

331

I have a great sense of humour.

332

"Laughter is a sunbeam of the soul."

Thomas Mann

333

"We don't LAUGH because we're HAPPY – we're HAPPY because we LAUGH."

William James

334

"Surround YOURSELF with people who make your HEART smile. It's then, only then, that you'll find WONDERLAND."

I love to LAUGH. 335

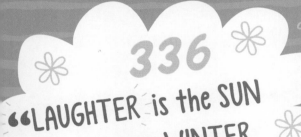

336
"LAUGHTER is the SUN that drives WINTER from the HUMAN FACE."

Victor Hugo

NATURE'S JOY ♪

337 Get out into nature today and take a close look at just how amazing it is. Take a really close look at the inside of a flower, the bark of a tree, a ladybird or a spider's web. How does it make you feel?

338

"The world is mud-luscious and puddle-wonderful."
E. E. Cummings

339

Time I spend in nature makes me happy.

340

"The earth has music for those who listen."

William Shakespeare

341

"I took a WALK in the WOODS and came out TALLER than the TREES."

Henry David Thoreau

I can see the wonder in NATURE. 342

343 "The EARTH laughs in FLOWERS."

Ralph Waldo Emerson

Making Things Better

☆ **344**

Can you think about something that was hard for you in the past that got better – what did you do? Did you try again? Did a friend help you? Did you talk it over? Did you try something new? You can always make things a little better than they are. It is really helpful to remember you have the power to change things.

345
I can make things BETTER.

346
"Shared joy is a double joy; shared sorrow is half a sorrow."

Swedish proverb

347

"If you can't find the ☆ **SUNSHINE** BE the ★ **SUNSHINE**

"The secret of change is **348** to focus all of your energy, not on fighting the old, but on building the new. " ☆ *Socrates*

☆ I can **349**
ASK FOR HELP
when I need it. ☆

"If life gives you
LEMONS
350 make lemonade!" ☆

MUSIC

351

Music is a brilliant way to change your mood. Can you put together a playlist of happy songs? Ask people for suggestions so you find some new ones too.

352

I dance and sing to make MYSELF HAPPY.

353

"Music is the strongest form of magic."

Japanese proverb

354

"I don't sing because I'm HAPPY; I'm HAPPY because I SING."

William James

355

"A great song should lift your heart, warm the soul and make you feel good."

Colbie Caillat

I am grateful for the music I hear. ✽ 356

357

" Life is one grand, sweet song so start the music. "
Ronald Reagan

It's a Wonderful Life

* 358

Write, draw, or tell somebody about something wonderful that has happened to you. Reliving something wonderful makes it doubly good.

359
I LOVE life
and life
LOVES
me.

360
"This is a wonderful
day. I've never seen
this one before."
Maya Angelou

361

"Begin doing what **YOU WANT** to do now... We have only this moment, **SPARKLING** like a **STAR** in our hand and melting like a snowflake." ☆

Francis Bacon

"Be HAPPY, and a reason will come ALONG." 362

I believe that life can be 363 WONDERFUL.

"The biggest ADVENTURE you can ever take is to live the life of your dreams."
Oprah Winfrey 364

☆ **365**

Take some time today to reflect back on the year and your HAPPIEST MOMENTS. What is your HAPPIEST MEMORY from the YEAR gone by? What HAPPY EVENT are you most looking forward to in the coming YEAR?

Every 4 years is a leap year so here is one extra for you!

"The sky is full of stars and there's room for them all to shine."

Acknowledgements

32 Montgomery, L.M., *Anne of Green Gables*, L.C. Page & Co (1908)

58 Whitman, Walt, 'A Song for Occupations', *Leaves of Grass* (1855)

60 Dickinson, Emily, 'Forever © is composed of Nows © (690)', *The Poems of Emily Dickinson* Harvard University Press (1999)

81 Dahl, Roald, *The Twits*, Jonathan Cape (1980)

93 Whitman, Walt, 'Song of Myself, 3', *Leaves of Grass* (1855)

115 Dr. Seuss, *Happy Birthday to You!*, Random House (1959)

117 *Winnie the Pooh: Sing a Song with Pooh Bear*, © Walt Disney Pictures (1999)

130 Hurston, Zora Neale, *Their Eyes Were Watching God*, HarperCollins (1937)

132 Comden, Betty and Green, Adolph, 'Never Never Land'
from *Peter Pan* (1954)

158 Alcott, Louisa May, *Little Women*, Little, Brown (1868)

159 *Pooh's Grand Adventure: The search for Christopher Robin* ©
Walt Disney Pictures (1997)

180 Alcott, Louisa May, *Little Women*, Little, Brown (1868)

250 Milne, A.A., *Winnie-the-Pooh*, Egmont (1926)

265 Dr. Seuss, *One Fish, Two Fish, Red Fish, Blue Fish*, Random House (1960)

305 Baum, L. Frank, *The Wonderful Wizard of Oz*,
George M. Hill Company (1900)

336 Hugo, Victor, *Les Misérables*, (1862)